Reading-literature

THE READING-LITERATURE SERIES

THE FIRST READER

READING-LITERATURE

FIRST READER

ADAPTED AND GRADED

BY

HARRIETTE TAYLOR TREADWELL

PRINCIPAL, WEST PULLMAN SCHOOL, CHICAGO

AND

MARGARET FREE

PRIMARY TEACHER, FORESTVILLE SCHOOL, CHICAGO, 1898-1908

ILLUSTRATED BY

FREDERICK RICHARDSON

ROW, PETERSON & COMPANY

EVANSTON, ILLINOIS

NEW YORK PHILADELPHIA SAN FRANCISCO

PREFACE

For years the most progressive educators have been urging that only good literature should be used in school readers. Some authors of primers and first readers have thought it impossible to provide such material within the vocabulary that beginners can learn with ease. Others have used a little real literature with a large amount of unrelated and uninteresting material specially prepared for the sake of word repetition and phonic drill.

Experience proves that all children are interested in and enjoy the simple folk tales, which are the literary products of many minds, and which have survived the centuries because they represent universal human experiences and satisfy certain common needs of childhood. Through countless repetitions, from one generation to another, they have assumed a form marked by simplicity and literary charm.

Equally interesting and wholesome are the nursery rhymes and jingles by Mother Goose, Christina G. Rossetti and others. After the Primer has been mastered, these bits of language-play, interspersed in little groups among the stories, add much to the delight of a child's reading book.

THE AUTHORS.

CONTENTS

CONTENTS

CONTENTS

TO LITTLE CHILDREN
LEARNING TO READ

The Three Little Pigs

Once upon a time there were
three little pigs.
One morning the mother said,
"You must go out
and make your living."
So they all set out.

The first little pig met a man
with some straw.
He said, "Please give me some straw,
I want to build a house."
The man gave the little pig some straw.
Then the little pig made a house.

Soon an old wolf came along.
He knocked at the door and said,
"Little pig, little pig, let me come in."

The little pig said,
"No, no, by the hair
of my chinny, chin, chin.
I won't let you in."

The wolf said,
"Then I'll huff and I'll puff,
and I'll blow your house in."

So he huffed and he puffed,
and he blew the house in.
Then he ate up the little pig.

The second little pig met a man
with some sticks.
He said, "Please give me some sticks,
I want to build a house."
The man gave the little pig some sticks,
and he built a house.

Then the old wolf came along.
He knocked at the door and said,
"Little pig, little pig, let me come in."

The little pig said,
"No, no, by the hair
of my chinny, chin, chin.
I won't let you in."

The wolf said,
"Then I'll huff and I'll puff,
and I'll blow your house in."
So he huffed and he puffed,
and he blew the house in.
Then he ate up the little pig.

The third little pig met a man
with some bricks.
He said, "Please give me some bricks,
I want to build a house."
The man gave the little pig some bricks,
and he built a house.

Then the old wolf came along.
He knocked at the door and said,
"Little pig, little pig, let me come in."
The little pig said,
"No, no, by the hair
of my chinny, chin, chin.
I won't let you in."

"Then I'll huff and I'll puff,
and I'll blow your house in,"
said the wolf.

"You may huff and you may puff,
but you can not blow my house in,"
said the little pig.

The wolf huffed and he puffed,
and he huffed and he puffed.
But he could not blow the house in.

Then the wolf said, "Little pig,
I know of a fine field of turnips."

"Where is it?" said the pig.

"Down in the field," said the wolf.
"Will you go with me?
I will call for you in the morning.
Then we can get some for dinner."

"I will be ready," said the pig.
"What time shall we go?"

"At six o'clock," said the wolf.

The little pig got up at five o'clock,
and he went to the field.
He got some turnips and ran home.

The wolf came at six o'clock.
He knocked at the door and said,
"Little pig, are you ready?"

"I went at five o'clock," said the pig,
"and I have a pot full of turnips."

The wolf was angry, but he said,
"Little pig, I know of a fine apple-tree."

"Where is it?" said the pig.

"Down in the garden," said the wolf.
"Will you go with me in the morning?
I will come at five o'clock.
Then we can get some apples."

"I will go," said the pig.

This time the little pig got up
at four o'clock.
He went to the garden,
and filled his bag with apples.
He was getting down,
when he saw the wolf.

The wolf was very angry, but he said,
"Little pig, are the apples good?"

"Very good," said the little pig.
"Let me throw you some."

The pig threw the apples far away.
The wolf ran to get them.
Then the little pig ran home.

The next day the wolf came again and said,
"Little pig, let us go to the fair."

"I will go in the morning," said the pig.
"What time shall we go?"

"Let us go at three o'clock," said the wolf.

The next morning the pig got up
at two o'clock.
He went to the fair and got a churn.
He was going home when he saw the wolf.
The little pig was frightened.
So he jumped into the churn to hide,
and it rolled down the hill.
The wolf saw the churn rolling
down the hill.
He was frightened, too, and ran home.

Next morning the wolf went
to the little pig's house.
He said, "Little pig, I went to the fair.
I met a great round thing on the way.
It was rolling down the hill.
It frightened me and I ran home."

"I frightened you," said the pig.
"I went to the fair at two o'clock,
and I got a churn.
On the way home I saw you coming.
So I jumped into the churn,
and it rolled down the hill."

The wolf was now very angry.
"I shall come down the chimney," he said,
"and I shall eat you up."

The little pig made a fire.
He hung a pot of water over it.
Soon he heard the wolf coming
down the chimney.
He took the lid off the pot.
The wolf fell into it.

And the little pig had a good supper.

—*English Folk Tale*

The Cat and the Mouse

Once there was a cat and a mouse.
They lived in the same house.
The cat bit the mouse's tail off.
"Pray, puss," said the mouse,
"give me my long tail again."

"No," said the cat,
"I will not give you your tail
till you bring me some milk."

First she leaped,
And then she ran,
Till she came to the cow,
And thus she began:

"Pray, cow, give me some milk for the cat.
Then she will give me my long tail again."

"No," said the cow,
"I will give you no milk
till you bring me some hay."

First she leaped,
And then she ran,
Till she came to the farmer,
And thus she began:

"Pray, farmer, give me some hay
for the cow.
Then she will give me some milk
for the cat,
And then the cat will give me
my long tail again."

"No," said the farmer,
"I will give you no hay
till you bring me some meat."

First she leaped,
And then she ran,
Till she came to the butcher,
And thus she began:

"Pray, butcher, give me some meat
for the farmer.
Then he will give me some hay
for the cow,
The cow will give me some milk
for the cat,
And then the cat will give me
my long tail again.

"No," said the butcher,
"I will give you no meat
till you bring me some bread."

First she leaped,
And then she ran,
Till she came to the baker,
And thus she began:

"Pray, baker, give me some bread
for the butcher.
Then he will give me some meat
for the farmer,
The farmer will give me some hay
for the cow,

The cow will give me some milk
for the cat,
And then the cat will give me
my long tail again."

"Yes," said the baker,
"I will give you some bread.
But if you eat my flour,
I will cut off your head."

The baker gave the mouse some bread,
and she took it to the butcher.
The butcher gave the mouse some meat,
and she took it to the farmer.
The farmer gave the mouse some hay,
and she took it to the cow.
The cow gave the mouse some milk,
and she took it to the cat.
And then the cat gave the mouse
her long tail again.

– *English Folk Tale.*

Little Boy Blue

Little Boy Blue, come blow your horn,
The sheep's in the meadow,
    the cow's in the corn.
Where's the boy
    that looks after the sheep?
He's under the haystack, fast asleep.
Will you wake him? No, not I;
For if I do, he'll be sure to cry.

— *Mother Goose.*

Baa, Baa, Black Sheep

Baa, baa, black sheep,
  Have you any wool?
Yes, I have, sir,
  Three bags full.

One for my master,
  And one for my dame,
And one for the little boy
  Who lives in the lane.

—*Mother Goose.*

Pussy Cat

Pussy cat, pussy cat, where have you been?
I have been to London to see the queen.
Pussy cat, pussy cat, what did you there?
I frightened a little mouse under her chair.

—*Mother Goose.*

Blow, Wind, Blow

Blow, wind, blow!
    and go, mill, go!
That the miller may
    grind his corn;
That the baker may take it,
And into rolls make it,
And send us some hot
    in the morn.

—*Mother Goose.*

If All the World Were Apple-pie

If all the world were apple-pie,
  And all the sea were ink,
And all the trees were bread and cheese,
  What should we have to drink?

—*Mother Goose.*

Once I Saw a Little Bird

Once I saw a little bird
  Come hop, hop, hop;
So I cried, "Little bird,
  Will you stop, stop, stop?"

I went to the window
  To say, "How do you do?"
But he shook his little tail,
  And far away he flew.

—*Mother Goose.*

A Little Sister

I have a little sister;
  they call her Peep, Peep.
She wades in the water
  deep, deep, deep;

She climbs the mountains,
  high, high, high—
Poor little thing!
  She has but one eye.

—*Mother Goose.*

The Old Woman Under the Hill

There was an old woman
  lived under a hill;
And if she's not gone,
  she lives there still.

—*Mother Goose.*

Some Little Mice

Some little mice sat in a barn to spin,
Pussy came by, and put her head in;
"Shall I come in and cut your threads?"
"No, Miss Puss, you will bite off our
heads."

—Mother Goose.

Hush-a-bye Baby

Hush-a-bye, baby, on the tree top,
When the wind blows, the cradle will rock,
When the bough breaks, the cradle will fall,
Down will come baby, cradle, and all.

—Mother Goose.

The North Wind

The north wind doth blow,
And we shall have snow,
And what will the robin do then,
poor thing?

He'll sit in a barn,
And keep himself warm,
And hide his head under his wing,
poor thing!

The north wind doth blow,
And we shall have snow,
And what will the bee do then,
    poor thing?

In his hive he will stay,
Till the cold's passed away,
And then he'll come out in the spring,
    poor thing!

The north wind doth blow,
And we shall have snow,
And what will the dormouse do then,
    poor thing?

Rolled up in a ball,
In his nest snug and small,
He'll sleep till warm weather comes back,
    poor thing!

— *Mother Goose.*

The Bremen Band

Donkey: I am getting old,
I can not work.
My master wants to kill me.
What shall I do?
I will run away.
But how can I make a living?
I have a good voice.
I shall go to Bremen.
Then I can sing in the band.

Donkey: Good morning, Old Whiskers.
Why are you so sad to-day?

Cat: How can I be happy?
I am getting old,
I can not catch mice.
My master wants to kill me.
What shall I do?

Donkey: Come with me to Bremen.
You have a good voice.
You can sing in the band.

Cat: Yes, I will go with you.

Donkey: Good morning, old dog.
What are you doing here?
Why do you pant so?

Dog: I am getting old,
I can not work.
My master is going to kill me,
so I have run away.
But how can I make my living?

Donkey: Come with us to Bremen.
We can all sing in the band.

Dog: Yes, I will go with you.

Donkey: Good morning, Red Cock.
Why do you crow so loud?

Cock: Cock-a-doodle-do! cock-a-doodle-do!
Company is coming to-night,
I heard the cook say.
They want me for supper,
so I crow while I can.

Donkey: Will you come with us to Bremen?
You have a good voice.
You can sing in our band.

Cock: Yes, I will go with you.

Donkey: It is a long way to Bremen.
Let us sleep in the woods to-night.
I shall sleep under the tree.

Dog: I shall sleep under the tree, too.

Cat: I shall sleep on the branches.

Cock: I shall sleep on the branches, too.
Oh! I see a light in a house.

Donkey: Let us go to the house.

Dog: Yes, let us go to the house.

Donkey: I can see in the window.

Cock: What do you see, gray horse?

Donkey: What do I see?
I see a table, full of good food.
There are robbers at the table.

Dog: That shall be our supper.

Cat: Yes, that shall be our supper.
How can we get it?

Cock: We must drive the robbers away.
How can we do it?

Donkey: We can all sing,
and the robbers will run away.
I can sing,
Hee-haw! hee-haw! hee-haw!

Dog: I can sing,
Bow-wow! bow-wow! bow-wow!

Cat: I can sing,
Mee-ow! mee-ow! mee-ow!

Cock: I can sing, Cock-a-doo-dle-do!
cock-a-doo-dle-do!

Donkey: I will stand by the window.
Old dog, stand on my back.
Old Whiskers, get on the dog's back.
Red Cock, get on the cat's back.

Now, let us all sing together.
Ready, one, two, three.

All: Hee-haw! hee-haw! hee-haw!
Bow-wow! bow-wow! bow-wow!
Mee-ow! mee-ow! mee-ow!
Cock-a-doo-dle-do! cock-a-doo-dle-do!

Robber: Did you hear that noise?
It must be goblins.
Let us run away.

Cock: See the robbers run.
Come, let us eat their supper.

Dog: This is better than a bone.

Cock: We shall never be hungry again.

Donkey: I can eat no more.
Let us go to sleep.
I shall sleep under the tree.
Old dog, you sleep by the door.
Old Whiskers, you sleep by the fire.
Red Cock, you sleep on the roof.

Robber: It is all still now.

The goblins are gone.
Let us go back.

Cat: Spit, spit! I will scratch!

Robber: Let me out, let me out!
An old goblin is scratching me.

Dog: Bow-wow! I will bite!

Robber: A man has cut me with a knife.
Let me out! O, let me out!

Donkey: Hee-haw! I will kick!

Robber: A big goblin has struck me.

Cock: Cock-a-doo-dle-do! cock-a-doo-dle-do!

Robber: The judge on the roof says,
"Bring the robbers here."
Come, let us be off.

Donkey: We will not go to Bremen.
We will all live in this house.

Cock: Cock-a-doo-dle-do! cock-a-doo-dle-do!

—*German Folk Tale.*

Wee Robin's Christmas Song

Wee Robin Redbreast hopped upon a bush.
An old gray pussy came by and said,
"Where are you going, Wee Robin?"

Wee Robin said, "I'm going to the king.
I shall sing him a song
this good Christmas morning."

Gray pussy said, "Come here, Wee Robin,
I will show you a bonny ring
round my neck."

But Wee Robin said, "No, no, Gray Pussy!
No, no, you worried the wee mouse,
but you can not worry me."
So Wee Robin flew away.

Then Wee Robin came to a mud wall.
There he saw a gray hawk.
The gray hawk said,
"Where are you going, Wee Robin?"

Wee Robin said, "I am going to the king.
I shall sing him a song
this good Christmas morning."

Gray hawk said, "Come here, Wee Robin,
I will show you a bonny feather
in my wing."

But Wee Robin said, "No, no, Gray Hawk!
No, no, you pecked the wee linnet,
but you can not peck me."
So Wee Robin flew away.

Then Wee Robin came to a hole in a cliff.
There he saw a sly fox.
The sly fox said,
"Where are you going, Wee Robin?"

Wee Robin said, "I am going to the king.
I shall sing him a song
this good Christmas morning."
The sly fox said, "Come here, Wee Robin,
I will show you a bonny spot
on my tail."

But Wee Robin said, "No, no, sly fox!
No, no, you worried the wee lamb,
but you can not worry me."
So Wee Robin flew away.

Then Wee Robin came to a spring.
There he saw a wee lad getting a drink.

And the wee lad said,
"Where are you going, Wee Robin?"

Wee Robin said, " I am going to the king.
I shall sing him a song
this good Christmas morning."

The wee lad said, "Come here, Wee Robin,
I will give you some crumbs."

But Wee Robin said, "No, no, wee lad!
No, no, you hit the little sparrow,
but you can not hit me."
So Wee Robin flew away.

Then Wee Robin came to the king's castle.
There he saw the king and queen.
"Now I shall sing my Christmas song,"
said Wee Robin.

So Wee Robin sang
his good Christmas song.

Then the king said,
"What can we give Wee Robin
for his bonny Christmas song?"

"We can give him Jenny Wren
for a wife," said the queen.

So Wee Robin and Jenny Wren
flew away home.

—*Scotch Folk Tale.*

The Straw Ox

A long time ago there was an old man
and an old woman.
They were very poor.
The old man worked in the field.
And the old woman spun flax.

One day the old woman said,
"Daddy, make me a straw ox,
and smear it with tar."

"What is the good of a straw ox?"
said the old man.

"Please make me a straw ox,"
said the old woman.

So the old man made the straw ox,
and he smeared it with tar.

The next morning the old woman drove
    the straw ox into the field.
She said, "Graze away, little ox,
    while I spin my flax."

She spun her flax a long time.
Then she fell asleep.

Soon a bear came out of the woods.
He ran at the ox and said,
  "Who are you? Speak and tell me."

"I am an ox, I am.
I am made of straw
    and smeared with tar, I am."

"Oh," said the bear,
    "you are made of straw
        and smeared with tar, are you?
Give me some straw and tar.
Then I can mend my torn fur."

"You may take some," said the ox.

The bear ran at the ox.
He began to tear away the tar,
and he stuck fast.
He pulled and pulled, but could not let go.
Then the ox dragged the bear home.

The old woman awoke.
"Where is my ox?" she cried.
"I will go home to see."
So she got up and ran home.
And there stood the ox and the bear.

She ran to the old man.
"Look," she cried,
"the ox has brought us a bear."
The old man threw the bear into the cellar.

The next morning the old woman drove the ox into the field again.
"Graze away, little ox," she said,
"while I spin my flax."
She spun her flax a long time.
Then she fell asleep.

Soon a wolf came out of the woods.
He ran at the ox and said,
"Who are you? Speak and tell me."

"I am an ox, I am.
I am made of straw
and smeared with tar, I am."

"Oh, you are made of straw
and smeared with tar, are you?"
said the wolf.

"Give me some of your tar.
Then I can smear my coat,
and the dogs can not tear me."

"You may take some," said the ox.

The wolf ran at the ox.
He began to tear away the tar,
and he stuck fast.
He pulled and pulled,
but he could not get away.
Then the ox brought the wolf home.

The old woman awoke.
"Where is my ox?" she cried.
"I will go home to see."
So she got up and went home.
There stood the ox and the wolf.

She ran to the old man.
"Look," she cried,
"the ox has brought us a wolf."
The old man came out
and threw the wolf into the cellar.

The next morning the old woman caught
a fox in the same way.
And the next morning she caught a hare.
The old man put them into the cellar.

Then he sat down by the cellar door
and began to sharpen his knife.

The bear said,
"Daddy, why do you sharpen your knife?"

"I am going to take your skin off.
I want a warm jacket for winter,
and the old woman wants a coat."

"Do not take away my skin, Daddy.
Let me go and I will bring you some honey."

"See that you do," said the old man.
And he let the bear go.

Then he sat down again,
and he began to sharpen his knife.

"Why do you sharpen your knife, Daddy?"
said the wolf.

"I am going to take your skin off.
I want a fur cap for winter."

"Do not take away my skin, Daddy.
Let me go, and I will bring you
a flock of sheep."

"See that you do," said the old man,
and he let the wolf go.

Then he sat down again
and began to sharpen his knife.

"Why do you sharpen your knife, Daddy?"
said the fox.

"I am going to take your skin off.
I want a fur collar for winter."

"Do not take away my skin, Daddy.
Let me go and I will bring you
a flock of geese."

"See that you do," said the old man,
and he let the fox go.

Then the old man began to sharpen
his knife again.
The little hare said,
"Daddy, why do you sharpen your knife?"

"I am going to take your skin off.
Little hares have warm fur.
I want some mittens for winter."

"Do not take away my skin, Daddy.
Let me go, and I will bring you
some turnips."
"See that you do," said the old man,
and he let the hare go.

The next morning the old woman said,
"Some one is at the door.
Let us go to see who it is."

They went to the door.
There stood the bear with the honey.
There stood the wolf with the sheep.
There stood the fox with the geese.
And there stood the hare with the turnips.

Now the old man and the old woman
have all they need.
And the straw ox stands in the sun.

— *Russian Folk Tale.*

The Boy and the Fox

A boy saw a fox asleep on a hillside.
The boy picked up a stone and said,
"I will kill this fox.
Then I shall sell the fur
and get some money.
I shall buy rye with the money,
and I shall sow the rye
in my father's field.

"The people will pass by the field.
They will see my rye and they will say,
'What fine rye that boy has.'

Then I shall say to them,
'Keep out of my rye field.'
But they will not obey.
Then I shall call to them,
'Keep out of my rye field.'
But still they will not obey.

Then I shall shout to them,
'Keep out of my rye field.'
And then they will obey me."

The boy called so loud
that the fox awoke.
The fox sprang to his feet,
and away he went to the woods.
So the boy did not get even a hair
from the tail of the fox.

—*Swedish Folk Tale.*

The Caterpillar

Brown and furry
  Caterpillar in a hurry;
Take your walk
  To the shady leaf, or stalk.

May no toad spy you,
  May the little birds pass by you;
Spin and die,
  To live again a butterfly.

— *Christina G. Rossetti.*

Mix a Pancake

Mix a pancake,
Stir a pancake,
  Pop it in the pan.

Fry a pancake,
Toss a pancake,
  Catch it if you can.

—*Christina G. Rossetti*

If a Pig Wore a Wig

If a pig wore a wig
  What could we say?
Treat him as a gentleman
  And say, "Good day."

If his tail chanced to fail,
  What could we do?
Send for a tailoress
  To get one new.

—*Christina G. Rossetti*

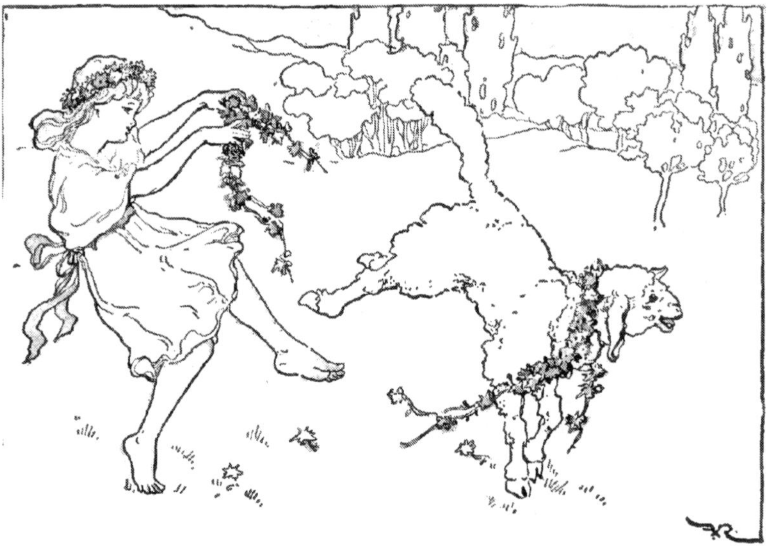

A Frisky Lamb

A frisky lamb
And a frisky child,
Playing their pranks
  In a cowslip meadow:
The sky all blue
And the air all mild,
And the fields all sun
  And the lanes half shadow.

— *Christina G. Rossetti.*

What They Do

What does the bee do?
    Bring home honey.
What does Father do?
    Bring home money.
And what does Mother do?
    Lay out the money.
And what does Baby do?
    Eat up the honey.

—*Christina G. Rossetti.*

The Lambkins

On the grassy banks,
  Lambkins at their pranks;
Woolly sisters, woolly brothers
  Jumping off their feet,
While their woolly mothers
  Watch by them and bleat.

—*Christina G. Rossetti.*

The Broken Doll

All the bells were ringing,
All the birds were singing,
When Molly sat down crying
    For her broken doll.

O you silly Moll!
Sobbing and sighing
    For a broken doll,
When all the bells are ringing,
And all the birds are singing.

— *Christina G. Rossetti.*

The Stars

What do the stars do
  Up in the sky,
Higher than the wind can blow,
  Or the clouds can fly?

—*Christina G. Rossetti.*

Wrens and Robins

Wrens and robins in the hedge,
  Wrens and robins here and there;
Building, perching, pecking, fluttering
  Everywhere!

—*Christina G. Rossetti.*

Sun-Loving Swallow

Fly away, fly away over the sea,
Sun-loving swallow, for summer is done;
Come again, come again, come back to me,
Bringing the summer and bringing the sun.

—*Christina G. Rossetti.*

The Town Mouse and the Country Mouse

A town mouse met a country mouse
in a forest.
The country mouse was getting nuts.
"Are you getting nuts for food?"
asked the town mouse.

"Yes," said the country mouse,
"I am getting nuts for winter.
The woods are full of nuts.
It is a fine place to live."

"I have a fine place to live too,"
said the town mouse.
"I do not get nuts for winter,
but I have all I want to eat.
You must come to see me."

"Yes, I will," said the country mouse.
"But you come to see me first.
You can come on Christmas."

So the town mouse went to see
the country mouse on Christmas.
It was a long way.
And there was snow on the ground.
So when the town mouse got there
he was very hungry.

The country mouse had nuts to eat,
and she had good water to drink.
The country mouse ate a big dinner.

But the town mouse said,
"I can not eat this food.
It is not good.
Now you come to see me,
and eat some of my food."

So the town mouse went home.
And the country mouse went with him.
It was a long way.
They were very hungry.

The town mouse had bread and cheese
and crumbs from the Christmas dinner.
The food was very good.
The country mouse ate and ate.
Then she said to the town mouse,
"How rich you must be."

Soon a door opened, and a woman came in.
The town mouse ran to his hole.
The woman went out
and left the door open.
A big, hungry cat came running in.

The town mouse ran far into his hole.
The country mouse ran after him.
But the old cat caught the country mouse
by the tail.

Then the door shut with a bang.
This frightened the cat,
and she let go of the mouse.

The country mouse jumped far into the hole.

"Do you call this a happy home?
Do you call this riches?" said she.
"I do not want such riches.
I only got away with my life.
I am happy in my country home.
There I have nuts and good water.
And I do not have to run for my life.
Good day, I am going home."
And the country mouse ran home
as fast as she could.

—*Norse Folk Tale.*

Little Two Eyes

Once there were three little sisters.
The first sister had but one eye.
It was in the middle of her forehead
She was called Little One Eye.

The second sister had two eyes.
She was called Little Two Eyes.

The third sister had three eyes.
One eye was in the middle of her forehead.
She was called Little Three Eyes.

Little Two Eyes was not happy.
One Eye and Three Eyes made fun of her
They made her wear old clothes.
They gave her only crumbs to eat,
and she was always hungry.

They said, "You are not our sister.
You have two eyes.
You have no eye in the middle
of your forehead."

Little Two Eyes took care of the goat.
Every morning she drove it to the field.
She took crumbs with her to eat.

One morning she was very hungry,
and she began to cry.
She cried for a long time.
Then she heard a sweet voice,
and she looked up.
There stood a little old woman.

"Why are you crying, Little Two Eyes?"
she said.

"My sisters do not like me
because I have two eyes.
They make me wear old clothes,
and they give me only crumbs to eat.
I am hungry," said Little Two Eyes.

"Do not cry," said the old woman,
"you shall never be hungry again.
Say to your goat,
'Little goat, if you are able,
Pray deck out my little table.'
And a little table will stand before you
with good food on it.
You may eat all you want.
Then you must say,
'Little goat, when you are able,
Take away my little table.'
And the table will go away."
Then the old woman went away.

Little Two Eyes was very hungry.
So she said,
"Little goat, if you are able,
Pray deck out my little table."
Soon a little table stood before her
with a good dinner on it.

Little Two Eyes sat down
and ate all she wanted.
Then she said,
"Little goat, when you are able,
Take away my little table."
And the little table went away.

Little Two Eyes was very happy.
"That is a fine way to keep house,"
she said.
She did not eat the crumbs that night.

One day Three Eyes said,
"What does Little Two Eyes eat?
She does not eat our food."
"I will go to the field and see,"
said One Eye.

The next morning One Eye said,
"I will go to the field with you,
Little Two Eyes."

They drove the goat into the long grass.
Then Little Two Eyes said,
"Let us sit here, Little One Eye,
and I will sing to you."
So they sat down in the long grass.
And Little Two Eyes sang,

"Are you awake, Little One Eye?
Are you asleep, Little One Eye?
Are you awake?
Are you asleep?
Awake?
Asleep?"

Soon One Eye fell asleep.
Then Little Two Eyes said,
"Little goat, if you are able,
Pray deck out my little table."
And there stood the little table.
She ate a good dinner and said,
"Little goat, when you are able,
Take away my little table."
And the little table went away.

Then One Eye awoke.
"The sun has set," said Little Two Eyes.
Come, let us go home."

The next morning, Three Eyes said,
"I will go to the field with you."

They drove the goat into the long grass.

"Let us sit down and I will sing to you,"
said Little Two Eyes, and she sang,

"Are you awake, Little Three Eyes?
Are you asleep, Little Two Eyes?
Awake, Little Three Eyes?
Asleep, Little Two Eyes?
Awake?
Asleep?"

Soon her two eyes went to sleep.
But the eye in the middle
of her forehead did not go to sleep.

Little Two Eyes did not know this.

So she called for her table.
She ate her dinner,
and the table went away.

Three Eyes looked out of her open eye,
and she saw all that Little Two Eyes did.

"Come, Little Three Eyes, the sun has set,
let us go home," said Little Two Eyes.
So they went home.

Three Eyes said to Little One Eye,
"I know why she does not eat."
And she told her sister all about the goat
and the table.
So they went to the field
and killed the goat.

Then Little Two Eyes sat down and cried.
Soon the little old woman stood by her.
"Little Two Eyes, why do you cry?"
she said.

"I cry because my goat is killed,"
said Little Two Eyes.

The old woman said,
"Go home and get the heart of the goat.
Then plant it by the house."
Little Two Eyes ran to her sisters and said,
"Please give me the heart of the goat."

Her sisters laughed and said,
"You may have it.
We do not want it."

Little Two Eyes took the heart of the goat,
and she planted it in the ground.
That night a tree grew up from the heart,
and it was full of golden apples.

"How did the tree get there?" said One Eye.

"How could a tree grow up in one night?"
said Three Eyes.

But Little Two Eyes knew all about it.
When One Eye climbed the tree,
the apples sprang away from her.

"I can see better than you,
let me try," said Three Eyes.
So she climbed the tree,
but the apples sprang from her, too.

"Let me try," said Little Two Eyes.

"What can you do with two eyes?
This tree is not for you," said her sisters.

But Little Two Eyes climbed the tree,
and the apples fell into her hands.

"I can get them now," said Three Eyes.

"So can I," said One Eye.

Just then a prince rode up.
The sisters said to Little Two Eyes,
"Run away and hide.
The prince must not see you;
you have two eyes."
And they hid her under a keg.

The prince saw the sisters and the tree
with the golden apples.
"Please give me a golden apple," said he.

"We will get some for you,"
said the sisters.

So they climbed the tree, but the branches
sprang away from them.

"This tree is not yours," said the prince,
"you cannot get an apple."
"The tree is ours, it is ours,"
they said again and again.

Then Little Two Eyes rolled a golden apple
to the prince.

"Where did this come from?" said he.
Then she rolled another apple to him.
"I must see where they come from,"
said the prince.
He looked under the keg,
and there sat Little Two Eyes.
"Can you pick some apples for me?"
said the prince.

"Yes, I can," she said.
Then Little Two Eyes climbed the tree.

She got the golden apples
and gave them to the prince.
He looked at her and said,
"What can I do for you?"

"Take me away with you," she said,
"I am not happy here."
So the prince took her on his horse,
and they rode away.
He took her to his father's castle.

The next morning Little Two Eyes looked
out of the window.
There stood the tree with the golden apples.
Little Two Eyes was very happy.

—*Grimm's Fairy Tales.*

Little Half Chick

Once upon a time an old hen had
a large brood of chickens.
They were fine chickens.
But one little chick was very odd.
He had but one leg, and one wing,
and one eye.
So his mother called him "Half Chick."

Half Chick did not mind his mother.
She would call, "Cluck! Cluck!"
But Half Chick would run away and hide.

One day he said,
"Mother, I am tired of this farm yard.
I am going to see the King."

"It is a long way to the King's palace,"
said his mother.
"You are too little to go alone.
Do not go now,
and some day I will take you."

But Half Chick tossed his head and said,
"I shall go to-day."
And hippity-hop, away he went.

Soon Half Chick came to a brook.
The brook was full of weeds.
It said, "Please stop and help me,
Little Half Chick.
These weeds are choking me,
Please help me take them away."

But Half Chick tossed his head and said,
"I have no time to help you.
I am going to see the King."
And hippity-hop, away he went.

Soon Half Chick came to a fire.
The fire was nearly burned out.
It said, "Please stop and help me,
Little Half Chick.
Give me some sticks, or I shall die."

But Half Chick tossed his head, and said,
"I have no time to help you.
I am going to see the King."
And hippity-hop, away he went.

Soon Half Chick came to a large oak-tree.
The wind was caught in its branches.
"Stop and help me, Half Chick,"
said the wind.
"I can not get away from these branches.
They are holding me fast.
Please help me to get away."

But Half Chick tossed his head and said,
"I have no time to help you.
I am going to see the King."
And hippity-hop, away he went.

At last Half Chick came
to the King's palace.
"Now I shall see the King," said he.
But just then the King's cook saw him.

"This is just what I need," said the cook.
"The King wants chicken soup for dinner."
And the cook picked Half Chick up
and popped him into a pot of water.

"Water, water, please help me,"
cried Half Chick.
"I do not like to get wet."

But the water said,
"I was once the brook, Half Chick.
The weeds were choking me.
You would not help me then,
so I can not help you now."
Then the fire began to burn.

"Fire, fire, please help me.
Do not burn me," cried Half Chick.
And he hopped from one side of the pot to the other.

But the fire said,
"I was dying once, Half Chick,
and you would not help me.
So I can not help you now."

Just then the wind came by.
He caught Half Chick up,
and carried him up into the air.

"Thank you, Wind," said Half Chick.
"Please let me down now."

But the wind said,
"Once I was caught in an oak-tree.
The branches held me fast.
I could not get away,
and you would not help me.
So I can not help you now."

Then the wind blew him up
to the top of a steeple.
There Half Chick stuck fast.
And there you can see him to this day.
He stands on his one leg,
and he looks at the wind
out of his one eye.

—Spanish Folk Tale.

I Had a Little Pony

I had a little pony,
His name was Dapple-grey,
I lent him to a lady,
To ride a mile away;
She whipped him, she slashed him,
She rode him through the mire;
I would not lend my pony now
For all the lady's hire.

There Was a Crooked Man

There was a crooked man,
And he went a crooked mile,
He found a crooked sixpence,
Upon a crooked stile,
He bought a crooked cat,
Which caught a crooked mouse,
And they all lived together,
In a little crooked house.

—*Mother Goose.*

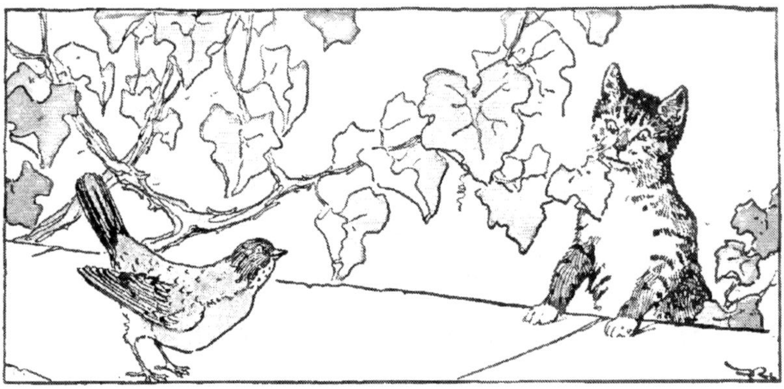

Little Robin Redbreast

Little Robin Redbreast sat upon a tree,
Up went Pussy Cat and down went he;
Down came Pussy Cat, away Robin ran,
Said little Robin Redbreast,
  "Catch me if you can."

Little Robin Redbreast jumped upon a wall,
Pussy Cat jumped after him,
  and got a little fall.
Little Robin sang and sang;
  and what did Pussy say?
Pussy Cat said, "Mew, mew, mew,"
  and Robin flew away.

—*Mother Goose.*

If all the Seas Were One Sea

If all the seas were one sea,
What a great sea that would be!
If all the trees were one tree,
What a great tree that would be!
If all the axes were one axe,
What a great axe that would be!
If all the men were one man,
What a great man he would be!
And if that great man took the great axe,
And cut down the great tree,
And let it fall into the great sea,
What a splash, splash, that would be!

—Mother Goose.

Simple Simon

Simple Simon met a pieman,
Going to the fair;
Said Simple Simon to the pieman,
"Let me taste your ware."

Said the pieman to Simple Simon,
"Show me first your penny;"
Said Simple Simon to the pieman,
"Indeed I have not any."

Simple Simon went a-fishing,
For to catch a whale;
All the water that he had
Was in his mother's pail.

He went to catch a dicky-bird,
And thought he could not fail,
Because he'd got a little salt
To put upon its tail.

—*Mother Goose.*

The Old Woman in a Basket

There was an old woman tossed up
in a basket,
Nineteen times as high as the moon.
Where she was going I couldn't but ask it,
For in her hand she carried a broom.

"Old woman, old woman, old woman,"
said I,
"O whither, O whither, O whither so high?"
"To brush the cobwebs off the sky!"
"Shall I go with you?" "Aye, by and by."

—*Mother Goose.*

Mother Hubbard

Old Mother Hubbard
  Went to the cupboard
To get her poor dog a bone;
  But when she got there
The cupboard was bare,
  And so the poor dog had none.

She went to the baker
  To buy him some bread,
But when she got back
  The poor dog was dead.

She went to the joiner
  To buy him a coffin,
But when she came back
  The poor dog was laughing.

She went to the hatter
  To buy him a hat,
But when she came back
  He was feeding the cat.

She went to the barber
  To buy him a wig,
But when she came back
  He was dancing a jig.

She went to the fruiter
  To buy him some fruit,
But when she came back
  He was playing a flute.

She went to the tailor
  To buy him a coat,
But when she came back
  He was riding a goat.

She went to the cobbler
  To buy him some shoes,
But when she came back
  He was reading the news.

She went to the hosier
  To buy him some hose,
But when she came back
  He was dressed in his clothes.

The dame made a courtesy,
  The dog made a bow,
The dame said, "Your servant,"
  The dog said, "Bow-wow."

—*M[illegible]e.*

Three Little Kittens

Three little kittens lost their mittens,
And they began to cry,
"O, mother dear,
We very much fear
That we have lost our mittens."

"Lost your mittens!
You naughty kittens!
Then you shall have no pie."
"Mee-ow, mee-ow, mee-ow."
"No, you shall have no pie."
"Mee-ow, mee-ow, mee-ow."

The three little kittens found their mittens,
    And they began to cry,
        "O, mother dear,
    See here, see here!
See! we have found our mittens."

"Put on your mittens,
    You little kittens,
    And you may have some pie."
"Purr, purr, purr,
    Oh, let us have the pie.
Purr, purr, purr."

The three little kittens put on their mittens,
    And soon ate up the pie;
        "O, mother dear,
    We very much fear
That we have soiled our mittens."

"Soiled your mittens!
You naughty kittens!"
Then they began to sigh,
"Mee-ow, mee-ow, mee-ow."
Then they began to sigh,
"Mee-ow, mee-ow, mee-ow."

The three little kittens washed their mittens,
And hung them out to dry;
"O, mother dear,
Do you not hear,
That we have washed our mittens?"

"Washed your mittens!
Good little kittens!
But I smell a rat close by!"
"Hush, hush! mee-ow, mee-ow!
We smell a rat close by!
Mee-ow, mee-ow, mee-ow!"

—*Mother Goose.*

Little Topknot

Once a cock and some hens lived
in a farm yard.
One little hen had a pretty topknot.
She was very proud of it.
So she strutted about by herself.
She wanted every one to see her topknot.

She would say, "Cluck, cluck, cluck!
See my pretty topknot."

One day she looked over the fence.
"Cluck, cluck, cluck!" she said.
"I am tired of this farm yard.
I want the world to see me.
I shall fly over the fence.
Cluck, cluck, cluck!
I want the world to see me."

The cock heard little Topknot.
He shook his comb and feathers, and said,
"Go not there! go not there!"
All the old hens said,
"Go-go-go! go not there!
Go not there! go not there!"

But little Topknot said, "Cluck, cluck!
I want the world to see me."
And she flew over the fence.
She felt very proud of herself.
So she strutted down the road.

Just then a hawk flew over her head.
He saw little Topknot all alone.
So he flew down
and he caught her in his claws.

The cock saw the hawk,
and he cried as loud as he could,
"Come, come, come and help!
Come and save Topknot."

The farmer heard the cock.
He came running out,
and he frightened the hawk away.

The hawk let Topknot go,
but he had her pretty topknot
in his claws.

Little Topknot was glad to get away,
and she ran back to the barn yard.
Soon she began to strut about.

Then the hens cried,
"Lost your topknot! Lost your topknot!"

Then little Topknot began to cry,
"See, see, see how I look!
See, see, see how I look!"

The cock came up to her.
He held his head very high and said,
"What did I tell you!
What did I tell you!"

Now Topknot does not strut about,
but she scratches for seeds.

—*Swedish Folk Tale.*

The Fisherman and his Wife

Once a fisherman and his wife lived
in a little hut by the sea.
One day the fisherman sat on the shore
with his rod.
"The fish do not bite to-day," he said.
Just then something pulled his line.
He drew up a large fish.

"Let me go," said the fish.
"I am not good to eat.
I am not a real fish.
I am an enchanted prince.
Please put me back into the water,
and I will swim away."

The fisherman put him back into the water,
and went home to his wife.

"Did you catch no fish to-day?"
said his wife.

"I caught a very large fish,"
said the fisherman.
"But it said to me,
'I am not a real fish.
I am an enchanted prince.
Put me back into the water,
and I will swim away.'

So I put it back into the water,
and it swam away."

"Did you wish for something?"
said his wife.

"What should I wish for?"
said the fisherman.

"You could wish for a pretty cottage,"
said she.
"I am tired of this little hut.
Go quickly and tell the fish
that we want a pretty cottage."

So the fisherman went back to the sea.
The water was all dark and green.
He stood by the shore, and said,
"O prince of the sea!
Come listen to me,
For my wife Isabel
Has a wish to tell."

The fish swam to the shore and said,
"What does she want?"
"She wants a pretty cottage," said he.
"She is tired of our little hut."

"Go home," said the fish.
"Your wife is in her cottage now."

The man went home.
There stood his wife at the cottage door
She took him by the hand and said,
"Come and see our cottage."
There was a pretty little parlor,
and a bedroom and a kitchen.
There was a little yard
with ducks and chickens.
And there was a little garden.

"Is this not beautiful?" said the wife.

"We shall always be happy now,"
said the fisherman.

But one day his wife said,
"This cottage is too small.
I want a large castle.
Go quickly and tell the fish."

So he went back to the shore.
The sea was all purple and dark blue.
The fisherman stood by it and said,

"O prince of the sea!
Come listen to me,
For my wife Isabel
Has a wish to tell."

"What does she want?" said the fish.

"She wants a large castle," said he.

"Go home," said the fish.
"Your wife is in her castle now."

The fisherman went home.
There stood his wife on the castle steps.

She took him by the hand,
and they went in.
There were large halls and beautiful rooms.
There were golden tables and chairs.
There was a garden
full of flowers and fruits.
And there was a forest
full of deer and sheep.

But his wife was not happy.
She wanted more power.
The next morning she said,
"You must be king of this country.
Go quickly and tell the fish so."

"I do not want to be king," said he.

"I will be queen then," said she.
"Go quickly and tell the fish
that I must be queen."

So the fisherman went back to the shore.
The sea was dark and gray.
There were great waves,
and they dashed upon the shore.
He stood by it and said,

"O prince of the sea!
Come listen to me,
For my wife Isabel
Has a wish to tell."

"What does she want now?" said the fish.

"She wants to be queen," said the man.

"Go home," said the fish.
"Your wife is queen now."

The man went home.
There he saw a great palace
with towers and gateways.
There were soldiers with trumpets
and drums.

He went in and there sat his wife
on a throne of gold.
His wife had a crown on her head,
and a wand in her hand.
The fisherman looked at her and said
"You are queen now.
We can wish for nothing more."
"I must have more power," said she.
"What shall it be?"

The next morning she said,
"What shall I wish for?"

The sun was just coming up.
She looked out of the window and said,
"I know what I want.
The sun must obey me,
and the moon must obey me.
They must rise and set
when I wish it."

So she went to the fisherman and said,
"The sun and moon must obey me!
Go quickly and tell the fish."

"I can not ask that," said he.
"The fish is angry,
and the sea is wild."
"Go," she cried, "I am queen,
and you must obey."

So he went back to the shore.

There was a great storm.
The sky was black.
The lightning flashed,
and the thunder roared.
The wind blew,
and the waves beat high.

The fisherman was frightened.
But he stood by the sea and shouted.

"O prince of the sea!
Come listen to me,
For my wife Isabel
Has a wish to tell."

"What does she want now?"
shouted the fish.

"She wants to rule the sun and moon.
She wants to tell them when to rise."

"Go home now," said the fish.
"You will find your wife in her hut."

The fisherman went home, and there sat his wife in the little hut.

And there they live to this very day.

—German Folk Tale.

The Lad and the North Wind

Once there was a poor woman.
She had one son.
One day he went to the safe for meal.
Along came the North Wind,
puffing and blowing.
He caught up the meal,
and away he went.

The lad went to the safe for more meal.
The North Wind came again.
He carried the meal off with a puff.
And he carried the meal off a third time.

Then the lad became angry.
"I will go to the North Wind," he said.
"I will ask him for my meal."
So off he went.

He walked and walked.
At last he came to the North Wind's house.
"Good-day, North Wind," said the lad.

"Good-day," said the North Wind.
"Thank you for coming to see me.
What do you want?"

"You took our meal yesterday.
Will you give it to me?" said the lad.
"We shall starve without our meal."

"I have no meal," said the North Wind.
"But I will give you this cloth.
You have only to say,
'Cloth, cloth, spread yourself,
and serve a good dinner.'
And you have all you want."

"Thank you, North Wind," said he.
And he set off for home.

It was a long way.
So he stopped at an inn.
He sat down at a table.
He took up the cloth, and said,
"Cloth, cloth, spread yourself,
and serve up a good dinner."
And the cloth did as it was bid.

The landlord saw the dinner.
"That is a fine cloth," he said.

Soon the lad went to bed.
The landlord took the cloth,
and he put another in its place.

Next morning the lad took the cloth
and went home.

"Mother," he said,
"I have been to the North Wind.
He is a good fellow.
He gave me this cloth.
I have only to say,
'Cloth, cloth, spread yourself,
and serve up a good dinner.'
And I have all I want to eat."

"That may be true," said his mother.
"But let me see it.
Then I shall believe it."

The lad drew out the table.
He laid the cloth and said,
"Cloth, cloth, spread yourself,
and serve up a good dinner."
But not a crumb did it serve.

"I must go back to the North Wind,"
said the lad.
And away he went.
He walked and walked.
At last he came
to the North Wind's house.

"Good-day, North Wind," said the lad.

"Good-day, lad," said the North Wind.
"Thank you for coming to see me.
What do you want now?"

"I want my meal," said the lad.
"This cloth is not worth a penny."

"I have no meal," said the North Wind.
"But you may have this ram.
You have only to say,
'Ram, ram, make money!'
And he will make all the money you want."

"Thank you, North Wind," said he.
And he set off for home.
It was a long way.
So he stopped at the inn.
He wanted some money.

So he said to the ram,
"Ram, ram, make money."
And the ram did as it was bid.

The landlord saw the money.
"That is a fine ram," he said.

Soon the lad went to bed.

The landlord took the ram,
and he put another in its place.

Next morning the lad took the ram
and went home.
"Mother," he said,
"I have been to the North Wind.
He is a fine fellow.
He gave me this ram.
I have only to say,
'Ram, ram, make money.'
And he makes all the money I want."

"That may be true," said his mother.
"But let me see it.
Then I shall believe it."

"Ram, ram, make money,"
said the lad.
But not a penny did he make.

"I must go back to the North Wind,"
said the lad.
And off he went.

It was a long way.
He walked and walked.
At last he came
to the North Wind's house.

"Good-day, North Wind," said the lad.

"Good-day, lad," said the North Wind.
"What do you want now?"

"I want my meal," said the lad.
"This ram is not worth a penny."

"I have no meal," said the North Wind.

"But I will give you this stick.
You have only to say,
'Stick, stick, lay on.'
And it will lay on till you say,
'Stick, stick, stop.'"

The lad took the stick.
"Thank you, North Wind," said he.
And he set off for home.

He stopped at the same inn.
After supper he shut his eyes
and began to snore.

The landlord saw the stick.
"That must be a fine stick," he said.

He thought the lad was asleep.
He reached for the stick.
Just then the lad cried out,
  "Stick, stick, lay on."
So the stick laid on.

The landlord jumped over tables and chairs.
He yelled and he roared.
"Lad, lad, stop the stick," he cried.
"You shall have your cloth
    and your ram again."

So the lad said,
  "Stick, stick, stop."

He took the cloth and the ram
    and the stick.
Then he set off for home.
So the North Wind gave the lad
    the worth of his meal.

—*Norse Folk Tale.*

The Sheep and Pig

Once there was a big fat sheep.
One morning the farm girl said,
"Eat, Sheep, for soon we shall eat you."

This scared the big sheep.
So he went to see the pig.
"Good-day, Pig," said the sheep,
"and thanks for our last merry meeting."

"Good-day, Sheep," said the pig,
"and the same to you."

"Do you know, Pig,
why they make you fat?"

"No, not I," said the pig.

"Then I will tell you," said the sheep.
"They are going to eat you."

This scared the pig.
"Let us go to the woods," he said.
"We can build a house to live in.
Then we shall have a home.
A home is a home, be it ever so lowly."

The pig said he would go,
so off they went.

When they had gone a bit of the way
they met a goose.
"Good-day, good sirs," said the goose,
"and thanks for our last merry meeting."

"Good-day, Goose," said the pig.

"Good-day, Goose," said the sheep.
"Whither away so fast to-day?"
said the goose.

"We go to the woods to build us a house.
A man's house is his castle."

"May I go with you?" asked the goose.

"What can you do, Goose?" asked the sheep.

"I can get moss to make the house warm."
Yes, they would let him go.

When they had gone a bit of the way,
a hare ran out of the woods.
"Good-day, good sirs," said the hare,
"and thanks for our last merry meeting.
Whither away so fast to-day?"

"Good-day to you," said the sheep.
"We go to the woods to build us a house.
There is no place like home."

"Oh!" said the hare,
"I have a house in every bush.
But I will go with you."

"What can you do?" said the pig.
"You can not build a house."

"Yes, I can," said the hare.
"I have teeth to gnaw pegs,
and I have paws to drive them.
I shall be the carpenter.
Good tools make good work."

So they all set off together.
Good company is such a joy.
When they had gone a bit of the way,
they met a cock.

"Good-day, good sirs," said the cock,
"and thanks for our last merry meeting.
Whither away so fast to-day?"

"Good-day, to you, Cock," said the sheep.
"We go to the woods to build us a house."

"What can you do, Cock?" asked the pig.

"Oh," said the cock,
"I will be the clock.
I will crow in the morning."
"Yes," said the pig,
"sleep is a great robber.
He steals half our lives.
We need you, Cock."

So they set off to the woods
    to build the house.
The pig cut the logs.
The sheep drew them home.
The hare put them together.
The goose picked moss
    and made the house warm.
And the cock crowed every morning.
So they all lived happily together.

It is good to go east and west,
    but after all home is best.

—Norse Folk Tale.

Mary Had a Little Lamb

Mary had a little lamb,
Its fleece was white as snow,
And everywhere that Mary went
The lamb was sure to go.

He followed her to school one day;
That was against the rule;
It made the children laugh and play
To see a lamb at school.

And so the teacher turned him out,
But still he lingered near,
And waited patiently about
Till Mary did appear.

"What makes the lamb love Mary so?"
The eager children cry,
"Oh, Mary loves the lamb, you know,"
The teacher did reply.

—*Sarah Josepha Hale.*

The Moon

O, look at the moon,
She is shining up there;
O mother, she looks
Like a lamp in the air.

Last week she was smaller,
And shaped like a bow,
But now she's grown bigger,
And round like an O.

—*Mother Goose.*

The Naughty Little Robin

Once there was a robin,
  Lived outside a door;
He wanted to go inside
  And hop upon the floor.

"Oh, no," said mother robin,
  "You must stay with me;
Little birds are safest
  Sitting in a tree."

"I do not care," said robin,
  And he gave his tail a fling.
"I do not think the old folks
  Know quite everything."

Down he flew, and kitty caught him
  Quicker than a wink:
"Oh," he cried, "I'm very sorry,
  But I did not think."

—*Phoebe Cary.*

What Does Little Birdie Say?

What does little birdie say,
In her nest at peep of day?
"Let me fly," says little birdie,
"Mother, let me fly away."

"Birdie, rest a little longer,
Till the little wings are stronger."
So she rests a little longer,
Then she flies away.

—Alfred Tennyson.

Twinkle, Twinkle, Little Star

Twinkle, twinkle, little star;
How I wonder what you are!
Up above the world so high,
Like a diamond in the sky.

When the blazing sun is set,
And the grass with dew is wet,
Then you show your little light,
Twinkle, twinkle, all the night.

In the dark blue sky you keep,
And often through my window peep;
For you never shut your eye
Till the sun is in the sky.

And your bright and tiny spark
Lights the traveler in the dark,
Though I know not what you are,
Twinkle, twinkle, little star.

—*Jane Taylor.*

WORD LIST

This list includes all of the new words in the Reading-Literature First Reader except those already used in the Primer. The words are arranged by pages in the order of their appearance.

1 upon
time
morning
mother
must
your
living
set
straw
build
house
2 soon
wolf
along
knocked
door
hair
chinny
chin
huff
puff
huffed
puffed
blew
3 second
built
4 third
bricks
5 may
could
fine
field
turnips
where
down
call
dinner
ready
6 six
o'clock
five
pot
full
angry
apple-tree
garden
apples
7 four
filled
bag
getting
when
very
throw
8 threw
far
fair
two
churn
going
frightened
jumped
hide
hill
rolling
too
9 round
thing
way
10 coming
chimney
hung
lid
off
supper
11 mouse
lived
same
bit
pray
puss
long
till
bring
milk
12 leaped
hay
13 meat
14 baker
15 flour
head
16 blue
sheep's
meadow
looks
haystack
asleep
wake
sure
17 baa
black
wool
yes
sir
master
dame
lives
lane
pussy cat
been
London
visit
queen
chair
18 wind
mill
miller
take
rolls
send

us
hot
morn
all
world
sea
ink
trees
should
have
hop
cried
window
20 sister
peep
wades
deep
climbs
mountains
high
poor
gone
still
21 mice
sat
barn
spin
threads
miss
hush-a-bye
baby
top
cradle
rock
bough
breaks
fall

22 north
doth
snow
robin
sit
keep
himself
warm
wing
23 hive
stay
cold's
passed
spring
dormouse
nest
snug
small
weather
back
24 Bremen
band
work
voice
25 whiskers
sad
catch
26 doing
here
pant
27 cock
crow
loud [dle do
cock-a-doo-
company
cook
29 branches

light
let
gray
table
food
robbers
30 drive
hee-haw
bow-wow
stand
31 together
32 hear
noise
goblins
bone
never
hungry
more
33 spit
scratch
scratching
knife
kick
struck
judge
roof
34 wee
redbreast
hopped
bush
Christmas
show
bonny
ring
neck
worried
worry

35 mud
wall
hawk
feather
pecked
36 linnet
peck
hole
cliff
sly
spot
lamb
lad
37 crumbs
hit
sparrow
castle
sang
38 wife
Jenny Wren
ago
39 worked
spun
flax
daddy
smear
tar
smeared
drove
40 graze
while
bear
speak
oh
mend
torn
fur

41 tear
stuck
pulled
dragged
awoke
stood
42 brought
cellar
next
43 coat
44 caught
hare
put
sharpen
45 jacket
winter
skin
honey
46 cap
flock
collar
geese
47 mittens
48 need
49 picked
stone
sell
buy
rye
money
father's
50 people
pass
obey
shout
sprang
feet

even	lambkins	running	cluck	men
51 caterpillar	woolly	61 bang	would	splash
brown	brothers	riches	76 tired	85 Simple
furry	jumping	such	farm-yard	Simon
hurry	watch	62 middle	tossed	pieman
walk	bleat	forehead	hippity-hop	taste
shady	55 broken	63 wear	weeds	ware
leaf	doll	clothes	help	penny
stalk	bells	always	these	indeed
toad	ringing	care	77 nearly	any
spy	singing	sweet	burned	a-fishing
52 mix	Molly	64 able	78 holding	whale
stir	crying	deck	79 now	pail
pop	silly	before	soup	dicky-bir
pan	Moll	69 called	popped	thought
fry	sobbing	open	wet	salt
toss	sighing	70 heart	80 other	86 basket
wore	56 higher	plant	dying	nineteen
wig	than	planted	81 steeple	carried
treat	hedge	grew	82 pony	broom
gentleman	building	golden	name	whither
chanced	perching	71 grow	Dapple-gray	brush
fail	pecking	about	lent	cobwebs
tailoress	fluttering	climbed	lady	aye
new	everywhere	hands	ride	87 Hubbard
53 frisky	sun-loving	72 just	mile	cupboard
playing	swallow	prince	whipped	bare
pranks	done	rode	him	none
cowslip	bringing	hid	slashed	88 joiner
air	57 town	keg	mire	coffin
mild	country	73 ours	lend	laughing
sun	forest	74 looked	hire	hatter
half	asked	took	crooked	feeding
shadow	nuts	75 large	bought	barber
54 does	place	brood	which	dancing
grassy	59 rich	chick	84 axes	jig
banks	60 opened	mind	axe	fruiter

fruit
flute
69 tailor
riding
cobbler
reading
news
hosier
hose
dressed
courtesy
servant
90 kittens
lost
much
fear
naughty
91 purr
soiled
92 sigh
washed
smell
close
hush
93 topknot
pretty
proud
strutted
94 fence
comb
95 claws
save
96 scratches
strut
97 fisherman
hut
shore

rod
something
drew
98 real
enchanted
99 wish
cottage
quickly
dark
green
listen
Isabel
has
100 swam
parlor
bedroom
kitchen
ducks
beautiful
101 purple
steps
102 halls
rooms
flowers
deer
power
103 waves
dashed
towers
soldiers
gateways
drums
trumpets
104 throne
crown
wand
nothing

105 rise
wild
106 storm
flashed
roared
lightning
beat
108 safe
meal
puffing
blowing
109 walked
starve
yesterday
without
cloth
spread
yourself
serve
110 stopped
inn
bid
landlord
another
111 fellow
believe
laid
112 worth
ram
116 shut
snore
117 reached
yelled
118 farm
girl
scared
merry

meeting
119 lowly
bit
120 moss
121 teeth
gnaw
pegs
paws
carpenter
tools
122 joy
clock
123 logs
happily
east
west
best
124 fleece
white
followed
school
rule
play
teacher
turned
lingered
near
patiently
appear
eager
reply
125 moon
shining
looks
like
lamp
last

week
smaller
shaped
bow
grown
bigger
126 outside
inside
floor
safest
sitting
fling
folks
everything
quite
Kitty
quicker
sorry
127 birdie
rest
longer
stronger
flies
128 twinkle
wonder
diamond
blazing
dew
often
through
bright
tiny
spark
traveller
though

PHONIC SERIES

For suggestions on the use of these series, see **Primary Manual, p. 63**

21
l eg
p eg
b eg
k eg

22
l ip
t ip
d ip
r ip
h ip
s ip
n ip

23
m ud
b ud

24
b ug
r ug
d ug
p ug
m ug
h ug
t ug

25
t ub
h ub
r ub

26
am
S am
h am
j am

27
c ob
s ob
m ob
r ob

28
r ag
w ag
b ag
t ag
s ag

29
ax
t ax
w ax

30
c ab
t ab

31
h im
d im
r im

32
f ix
s ix
m ix

Review

red
hen
cat
man
not
sob
pig
ox
it
will
dog
cut
did
met
run
tin
pup
rap
pad
leg
lip
bug
mud
tub
am
cob
rag
ax
cab
him
fix
rod

33
r od
G od
p od
h od
s od
n od

34
b e
m e
h e
th e
sh e
w e

35
m ake
b ake
sh ake
c ake
t ake
f ake
r ake
m ake
s ake
l ake

36
b ee
f ee
s ee
l ee
tr ee

37
t old
c old
b old
h old
g old
f old
s old
m old

38
g o
s o
n o

39
b ite
k ite
s ite
m ite

40
g oat
m oat
c oat
fl oat
b oat

41
c ane
p ane
m ane

42
ate
d ate
r ate
f ate
m ate
g ate
l ate
h ate

43
s ame
t ame
c ame
n ame
f ame
l ame
g ame

44
c ape
t ape

45
m ade
w ade
f ade

46
h ide
w ide
b ide
t ide
r ide
s ide

47
d ime
t ime
l ime

48
f ine
p ine
d ine
n ine
w ine
m ine
l ine

49
r ode
c ode
m ode

50
n ote
c ote
d ote
m ote
r ote

51
g ale
p ale
s ale
t ale

52
p ole
m ole
h ole
s ole

53
t une
J une

54
p ure
c ure

55
m ule
m ute

56
c ore
t ore
s ore
m ore
w ore

57
l ope
c ope
d ope
r ope
m ope
h ope

58
r age
p age
c age
s age

59
b ase
c ase
v ase

60
c ave
w ave

60
g ave
s ave
p ave

61
m ile
p ile
t ile
f ile

62
f ire
w ire
h ire
t ire

Review
be
make
bee
told
go
bite
goat
cane
ate
same
cape
made
hide
dime
fine
rode
note
gale
pole
tune
pure
mule

Review
core
lope
rage
base
cave
mile
fire
core

63
b ack
l ack
p ack
t ack
s ack

64
n eck
d eck

65
s ick
k ick
t ick
l ick
p ick

66
r ock
l ock

67
d uck
l uck
b uck

68
s ell
N ell

68
t ell
b ell
w ell
f ell

69
p uff
r uff
c uff
b uff
m uff

70
and
h and
s and
l and
b and

71
end
m end
b end
s end

72
b ent
s ent
r ent
w ent
t ent

73
t int
h int
m int
l int

74
r est
v est

74
t est
w est
b est
n est

75
f ist
m ist
l ist

76
r ust
m ust
j ust
d ust

77
c amp
l amp
d amp

78
b ump
p ump
j ump
d ump
l ump

79
f elt
b elt
w elt
m elt

80
g ift
s ift
l ift